PIANO • VOCAL • GUITAR

Top COUNTRY HITS

OF

2007-2008

STEALING CINDERELLA
CHUCK WICKS

OUR SONG
Taylor Swift

so small
carrie underwood

INTERNATIONAL HARVESTER
Craig Morgan

READY, SET, DON'T GO
Billy Ray Cyrus with Miley Cyrus

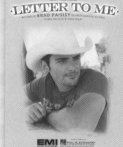
LETTER TO ME
Brad Paisley

CLEANING THIS GUN (COME ON IN BOY)
RODNEY ATKINS

As If
SARA EVANS

SMALL TOWN SOUTHERN MAN
ALAN JACKSON

HOW 'BOUT THEM COWGIRLS
GEORGE STRAIT

WHAT DO YA THINK ABOUT THAT
MONTGOMERY GENTRY

GET MY DRINK ON
TOBY KEITH, DEAN DILLON and SCOTT EMERICK

ALL-AMERICAN GIRL
Carrie Underwood

WINNER AT A LOSING GAME
RASCAL FLATTS

Watching Airplanes
GARY ALLAN

HOW LONG
Recorded by EAGLES
Words and Music by John David Souther

SUSPICIONS
TIM McGRAW

FIRECRACKER
Recorded by Josh Turner

DON'T BLINK
Recorded by Kenny Chesney

ISBN 978-1-4234-3706-2

HAL•LEONARD CORPORATION

7777 W. BLUEMOUND RD. P.O. BOX 13819 MILWAUKEE, WI 53213

Visit Hal Leonard Online at
www.halleonard.com

TOP COUNTRY HITS

ALL-AMERICAN GIRL

Words and Music by CARRIE UNDERWOOD,
KELLEY LOVELACE and ASHLEY GORLEY

Since the day
Six - teen,

they ___ got mar - ried, ___
short ___ years lat - er, ___

he'd been pray - in' for a
she was fall - in' for the

lit - tle ba - by boy. ___
sen - ior foot - ball star. ___

AS IF

Words and Music by SARA SCHELSKE,
HILLARY LINDSEY and JOHN SHANKS

11

CLEANING THIS GUN
(Come On In Boy)

Words and Music by CASEY BEATHARD
and MARLA CANNON-GOODMAN

DON'T BLINK

Words and Music by CASEY BEATHARD
and CHRIS WALLIN

FIRECRACKER

Words and Music by JOSH TURNER,
SHAWN CAMP and PAT McLAUGHLIN

Fast

When I

* *Recorded a half step lower.*

When I light the fuse, __ I got - ta get back quick. __ You
She goes off __ with __ a great big bang; __

got - ta be care - ful with a dyn - a - mite stick. Son of a gun, __ she's
boys, __ I tell __ you it's a beau - ti - ful thing. When she takes __ off, __ you bet - ter

fun to han - dle and she packs a punch __ like a Ro - man can - dle. She's a
hang on tight; __ she's a blonde bot - tle rock - et in the mid - dle of the night. When

We got a good thing go - in' and it feels so right.

She's a fire - crack - er, she's the light of my life.

Well, she's a fire - crack - er, she's the light of my

life.

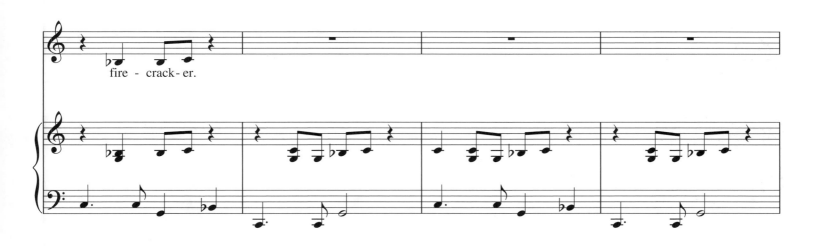

Fire - crack - er,

fire - crack- er.

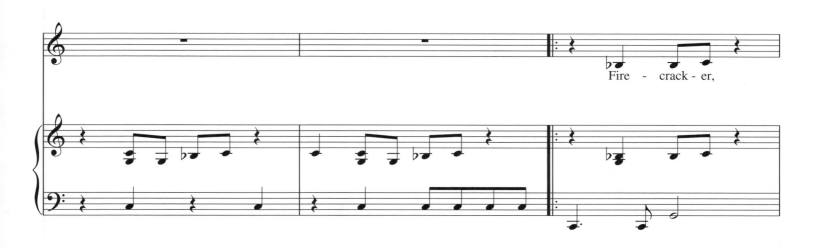

Optional Ending

C7

Repeat and Fade

GET MY DRINK ON

Words and Music by DEAN DILLON,
SCOTT EMERICK and TOBY KEITH

I'm gon-na get my drink ____ on. I'm gon-na hear me a

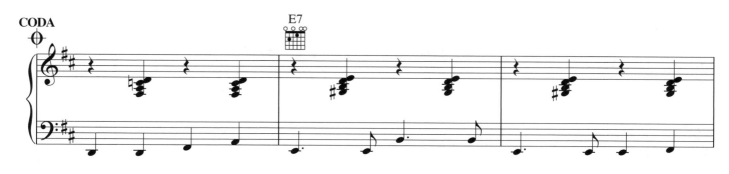

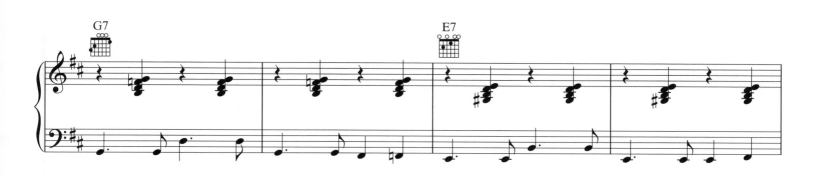

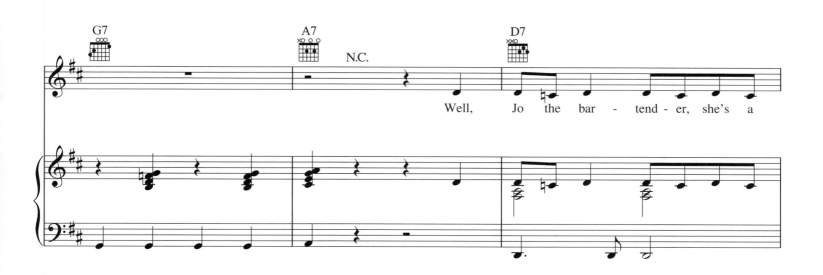

Well, Jo the bar - tend - er, she's a

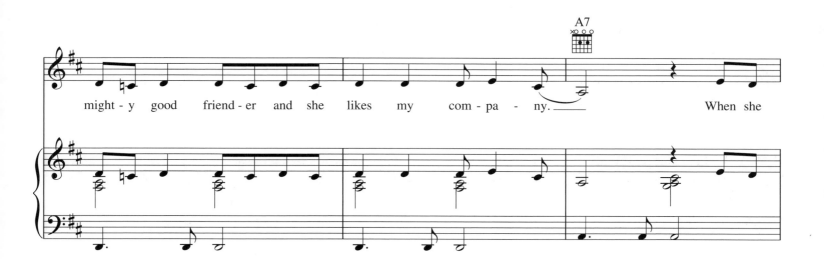

might - y good friend - er and she likes my com - pa - ny. _____ When she

HOW 'BOUT THEM COWGIRLS

Words and Music by CASEY BEATHARD
and ED HILL

HOW LONG

Words and Music by
JOHN DAVID SOUTHER

Moderately fast

Like a blue - bird _____ with his heart _____ re - moved, _

lone - ly as a train, _____ I've run just as far _

wish I lived _ in the land of fools ___ and no one knew my name. _

___ But what you get is not ___ quite what you

choose. _ Tell me how ___ long,

how ___ long, wom-an, will you weep? ___

INTERNATIONAL HARVESTER

Words and Music by SHANE MINOR,
DANNY MYRICK and JEFFREY STEELE

Moderately fast

I'm the son of a third gen-er-a-tion farm - er. I've been

married ten years to the farmer's daughter.

I'm a God-fearin', hard-workin' combine driver, hoggin' up the road on my p - p - p - p-plower, chug-ga-lug-ga-lug-gin' five miles an hour ____ on my In - ter - na - tion - al

Har - vest - er.

Three

Well, you may be on the state __ paved road, but that black - top runs through my __ pay - load. Ex - cuse me for try'n' to do __ my job, __ but this year ain't been __ no bump - er crop. __

LETTER TO ME

Words and Music by
BRAD PAISLEY

OUR SONG

Words and Music by
TAYLOR SWIFT

READY, SET, DON'T GO

Words and Music by CASEY BEATHARD
and BILLY RAY CYRUS

Moderately

Male: She's got-ta do ____ what she's ____ got-ta do ____ and I've ____ got-ta like it or not. ____
Female: Looks like ____ things ____ are fall - in' in place. *Male:* Feels ____ like they're fall-in' a - part. ____

SMALL TOWN SOUTHERN MAN

Words and Music by
ALAN JACKSON

Born the mid- dle son ____ of a farm- er and a small town South- ern man,

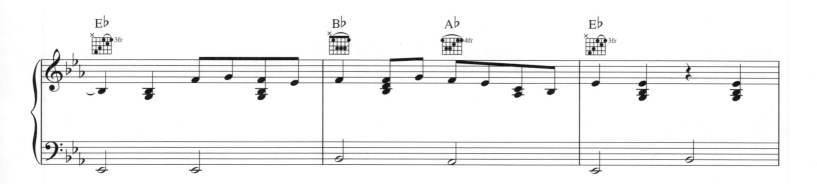

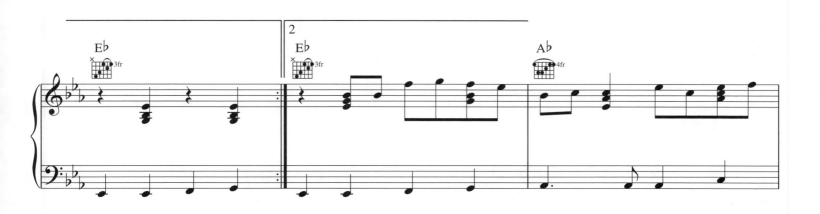

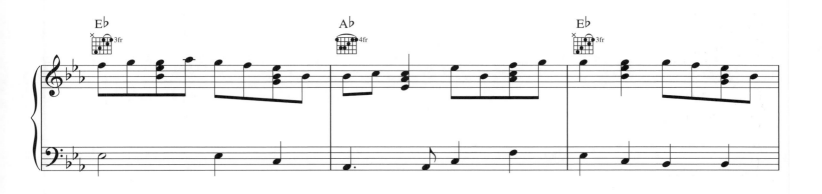

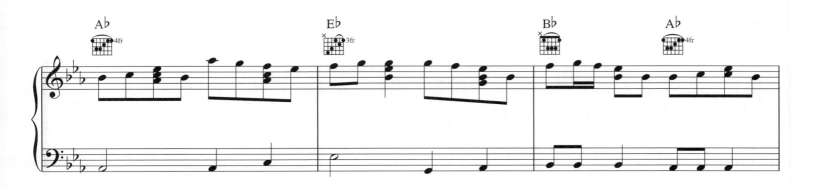

SO SMALL

Words and Music by LUKE LAIRD,
HILLARY LINDSEY and CARRIE UNDERWOOD

STEALING CINDERELLA

Words and Music by CHUCK WICKS,
RIVERS RUTHERFORD and GEORGE TEREN

SUSPICIONS

Words and Music by EVEN STEVENS,
EDDIE RABBITT, DAVID MALLOY
and RANDY McCORMICK

WATCHING AIRPLANES

Words and Music by JIM BEAVERS
and JONATHAN SINGLETON

Moderately

Sit - tin' out here on the hood ___ of this truck,
would -'ve lied, ___ could -'ve cried, ___ should have tried

look - in' up
hard - er,

at a car - a - mel - col - ored
done ___ an - y - thing ___ to

sun - set sky. ___
make you stay. ___

I'm
I won - der

*Recorded a half step higher.

WHAT DO YA THINK ABOUT THAT

Words and Music by RALPH SMITH
and BRETT JONES

heard it through the grape- vine my new neigh- bor don't like my big red
wear___ what I want to, o - ver- alls, work___ boots, crank my mu - sic up

134

WINNER AT A LOSING GAME

Words and Music by JAY DeMARCUS,
JOE DON ROONEY and GARY LEVOX

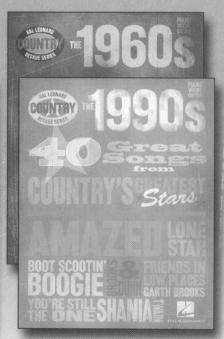